Complimentary Gifts

while you're in Savannah.

{presented by Wholesale Services of America}

Spend a few moments with us learning how you can save money on your next vacation by using Wholesale Services of America, and you could receive complementary tours, attractions, and gifts worth up to $300. Some qualifications apply.

GIVE US A CALL!
912.358.2059

© Donald J Pearson

Welcome

table of contents

© Fred Langley

© Bryan Stovall

© Donald Pearson

Fresh POP CORN

© Judi Trahan

© Old Fort Jackson

© Patrick McGhie

from the editor

© Casey Jones

"Behind the bricks and wrought iron fences are hidden gardens with landscaping and fountains that will take your breath away."

- Casey Jones, Photographer

Welcome to Savannah—you've arrived, and now you're looking to find out what to do. Whenever I travel, I love that sense of discovery. Maybe you're looking to discover something while you're in Savannah—a mouthwatering meal, your new favorite little black dress or your new understanding of how we do life down here in the South. With nearly three hundred years of history, Savannah awaits for you to discover her hidden gems.

This book, Savannah: A Southern Journey is all about letting you in on the treasures around Savannah. That's why I love our cover photograph this year. It peaks into a secret garden off Calhoun Square. There, we find a gorgeous fountain surrounded by cobbled pathways.

The photographer, Casey Jones is no stranger to capturing Savannah's beauty. As Visit Savannah's Content Marketing Manager, Jones snaps pictures and tells Savannah's stories every day. One of his favorite things to do might just be where you want to start your journey, "On a relaxing stroll through Savannah, you will likely spot one of our city's hidden gems. Behind the bricks and wrought iron fences are hidden gardens with landscaping and fountains that will take your breath away. Don't be afraid to take a peek. You'll like what you see in Savannah."

Let us help you get started with your southern journey in the pages of this book. Explore tips on where to dine, shop and experience Savannah. Find out what we, as locals, love to do. We welcome you with open arms!

Molly Swagler

Editor-in-Chief

On the cover: "Hidden Garden" photographed by Casey Jones

NONSTOP TO SOUTHERN SUNSETS: NOW BOARDING

SAVANNAH HILTON HEAD INTERNATIONAL

flySAV.com/NowBoarding

Out the Door & On Your Way

There's No Time to Waste

Let's Get You *Moving* on Your Southern Journey

Choose from Savannah's *tour & transportation options* to see all of the city's glorious sights with ease.

Whether you arrived via jet plane at Savannah-Hilton Head International Airport, rolled in on the highway or sailed in by boat, we extend our warmest welcome. As nice as your hotel room may be, you didn't come to Savannah to spend your whole time in there, right? So we say climb aboard! Let's get you out the door and on your way to exploring the remarkable scenery and sights of Savannah.

© Donald Pearson

Rest assured, there are so many stories in this city, surprises will await you at every turn!

© Tim Welch

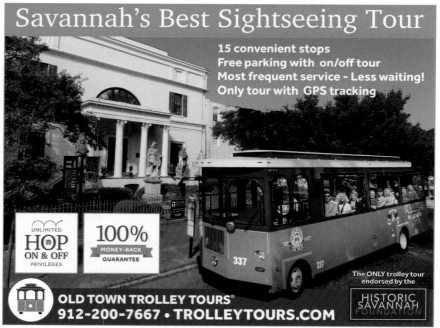

Savannah's Best Sightseeing Tour

15 convenient stops
Free parking with on/off tour
Most frequent service - Less waiting!
Only tour with GPS tracking

by *dot*.

Look for the plum-colored logo on buses and signs for fare-free transportation, in and around Savannah's beautiful Historic District. The dot gets you where you want to go, when you need to get there. You can also ride what the locals call the "CAT"—Chatham Area Transit. The CAT offers bike sharing, bus, paratransit, and ferry services throughout Chatham County.

by road.

It's always helpful to engage the services of a seasoned tour guide. For an open-air ride that hits all the important historical points from downtown through the historic district, a trolley is the way to go. Each has its own starting point and convenient parking lot and offers general Savannah tours as well as ghost tours, pirate tours, beach excursions and specialty services. Rest assured, there are so many stories in this city; surprises will await you at every turn!

by water.

If you're looking to spend some time on the water, try dolphin tours, sunset cruises and inshore and deep-sea fishing. Or, book a riverboat cruise for an evening of fine dining, captivating entertainment and a tour of Savannah from a unique perspective.

by wheel.

Prefer people-powered transportation? The three wheeled buggies of Savannah's pedi-cabs accommodate two people at a time for a breezy jaunt. Part bike, part modern rickshaw, these environmentally responsible vehicles are a favorite among bar-hoppers. The pedal pushers are happy to take you a few blocks or on a thorough tour down to Forsyth Park.

by foot.

There's bound to be some of you who would rather use the two feet you were born with to get around. Savannah is regularly named one of the best walking cities in America, and you only need to stroll for a couple of yards to figure out why—it's flat, mostly shady and there's always something to see.

{ Let's get you out the door and on your way to exploring the *remarkable scenery & sights* of Savannah. }

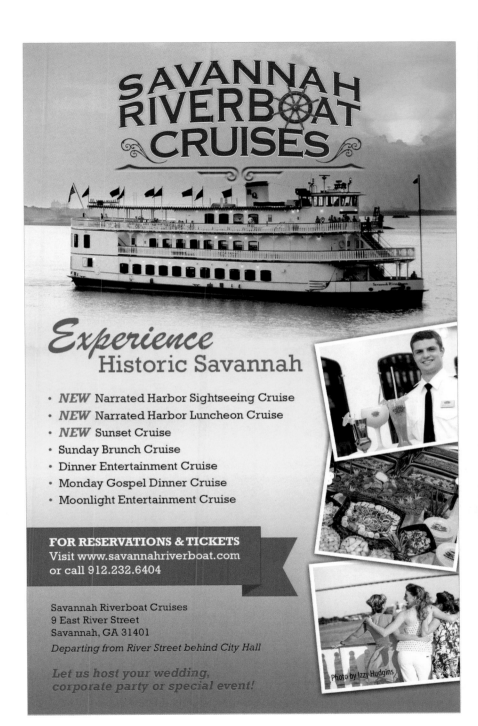

SAVANNAH RIVERBOAT CRUISES

Experience Historic Savannah

- *NEW* Narrated Harbor Sightseeing Cruise
- *NEW* Narrated Harbor Luncheon Cruise
- *NEW* Sunset Cruise
- Sunday Brunch Cruise
- Dinner Entertainment Cruise
- Monday Gospel Dinner Cruise
- Moonlight Entertainment Cruise

FOR RESERVATIONS & TICKETS
Visit www.savannahriverboat.com
or call 912.232.6404

Savannah Riverboat Cruises
9 East River Street
Savannah, GA 31401
Departing from River Street behind City Hall

Let us host your wedding, corporate party or special event!

Photo by Izzy Hudgins

Savannah 16

Atlanta ⇄ Savannah

- ✓ Daily Express Non-stop Departures
- ✓ First Class Shuttle Transportation
- ✓ Onboard Entertainment
- ✓ Complimentary Refreshments
- ✓ Free Wi-Fi and Power Outlets

WWW.SAVANNAH16.COM
Customer Service: 404.500.3966

© John Alexander Photography

© Kate Bagoy

© Fred Langley

© John Alexander Photography

© Chatham Area Transit

Riding a bicycle in our *vibrant downtown* means you are the driver of a vehicle. Be sure to adhere to all traffic laws.

BROUGHTON ST

Savannah's Historic Main Street

SHOP

Alton Lane	Kendra Scott
Banana Republic	Krewe Optic
bluemercury	Levy Jewelers
Club Monaco	Lilly Pulitzer
Copper Penny	L'Occitane
Dress Up Boutique	Lululemon
Free People	MAC
Gap	Michael Kors
Globe Shoe Co.	Modern Trousseau
Goorin Bros	Paris Market
H&M	Sperry Topsider
Half Moon Outfitters	Tommy Bahama
Impeccable Pig	Urban Outfitters
J. Crew	Victoria's Secret
J. Parkers	Vineyard Vines

EAT

B&D Burgers	Le Macarone
Beetnix Superfoods	Leopold's
& Juice Bar	McDonald's
Ben & Jerry's	Panera Bread
Blends: A Coffee	Ruan Thai Cuisine
Boutique	Savannah Bee
Broughton Market	Company
Chive	Savannah Seafood
Coffee Fox	Shack
Flying Monk	Savannah Taphouse
Noodle Bar	Smoothie King
Jalapenos	Spudnick
Kayak Kafé	Starbucks
La Berry	Subway
Frozen Yogurt	

Broughton Street blends Savannah's Southern charm and easy-going elegance with the emerging trends and style driven by specialty retailers, chef-driven restaurants and fashion-forward thinkers. The beautiful architecture and historic buildings that line the natural artery provide the perfect backdrop for a memorable experience.

See you on Broughton

BROUGHTON ST

broughtonstsavannah.com

Historic
BROUGHTON STREET

Savannah *Shopping*

One of the things we love to do in Savannah? Shop. From one-of-a-kind art pieces to handmade soaps, stores you love, stores you don't yet know and even rare antiques, there is certainly no shortage of options to find that perfect something. Here's a guide to some of our shopping districts.

Broughton Street.

From the beginnings of our city in 1733, Broughton Street has been our Main Street. Named after one of the carpenters who helped build this town, Broughton Street has always been the hub of shopping for Savannah. On this historic Main Street, you'll find brand names and local retailers you're sure to love. During the holidays, this street lights up the night sky in a big way.

Savannah Riverfront.

Find everything including Savannah books, Civil War artifacts, Southern gourmet selections, art, antiques *and more.*

< City Market.

Browse City Market's eclectic blend of art galleries and specialty shops that fill every nook and cranny of this part of the Historic District.

Greater Savannah.

Outside of the historic district, Savannah boasts two malls along with several outdoor shopping centers where you will find all of the brand names you love – *and more!* ❁

© Bryan Stovall

© Fred Langley

© Fred Langley

Dining
in SAVANNAH

© Angela Hopper Photography

The restaurant scene is as *diverse* and *storied* as the city itself. When it comes to dining in Savannah, bring your appetite, because *you owe it to yourself to taste it all*.

There's no doubt that Savannah's food scene has an endless array of mouthwatering temptations to please all appetites. From fine-dining establishments tailored to a romantic evening for two to the region's best down-home comfort food and – of course – fresh-caught, straight-from-the-ocean seafood.

Seafood is as much a part of Savannah as cobblestones, squares and Spanish moss. It is the official fare of locals and visitors alike, and other than a handful of specialty restaurants, you will be hard pressed to find an establishment in town that doesn't have something seafood on the menu.

© John Alexander Photography

Pork Brittany

CHARLESTON, SC • SAVANNAH, GA

39 RUE DE JEAN

BAR | CAFE

Flavor —
Intensified

FRENCH BAR AND BRASSERIE

SERVING DINNER NIGHTLY AT 5PM
605 W. OGLETHORPE AVE., SAVANNAH
39RueDeJeanSAV.com | 912.721.0595

She Crab Soup.

The Atlantic Blue Crab is the main ingredient in this creamy soup—also a Savannah staple dish. It doesn't matter if it's hot or cold outside, this rich soup will give you that downhome feel. And, there's a reason that it's the first on the menu at the famed Pirates' House restaurant. They've been making this southern tradition for a long time.

Fish from the Sea.

Grouper and flounder are found in abundance in Savannah's waters and their mild flavor and flaky white texture make them popular choices in most every restaurant. And, if you're looking for something fresh, try the Carolina Red Trout at 17hundred90. They pan-sear to perfection and top with the season's sides.

Oysters.

Sweet Savannah oysters are known for their intense salty flavor. From brackish shallow beds off the coast, oysterman harvest from October to May. Whether you prefer them raw, steamed, baked or fried, this coastal delicacy is sure to delight.

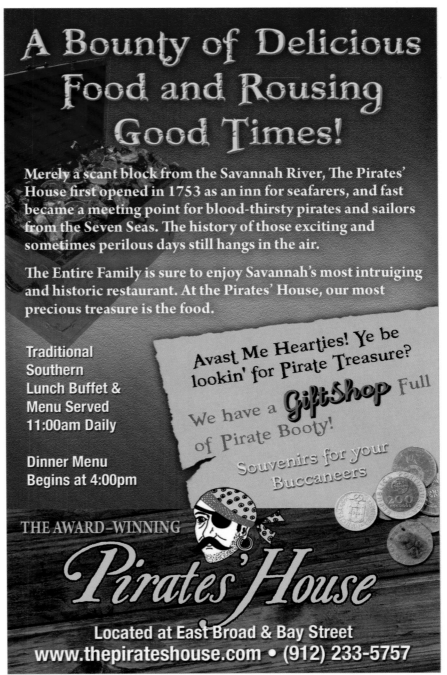

© Angela Hopper Photography

Shrimp & Grits.

Nothing says Savannah like freshly-caught Georgia shrimp and locally-grown grits—put them together for the perfect pair. You can find the pairing on most menus in town, but it's the variations we love to celebrate. At Belford's Savannah Seafood and Steaks, they add another Southern staple—greens. In a mouth-watering, three-part harmony, you'll find this simply southern shrimp, grits and greens in a chardonnay butter sauce with heirloom tomatoes.

Lowcountry Boil.

A dish heralding from our Gullah culture, the Lowcountry Boil is one of our favorites. The season's bounty boils in one pot and you pick, peel and eat with your hands. It's delicious. Try it at Barracuda Bob's Bar & Grill off of River Street.

Bouillabaisse.

You can elevate that Lowcountry Boil into a French fish soup, something more suited to a fine-dining date night. The best bouillabaisse in town is found at 39 Rue de Jean. They create a masterpiece for your mouth with local seafood and a white wine-saffron tomato broth. C'est manifique!

Whether seafood or international plates inspired by local flavor, *you're sure to fill your belly.*

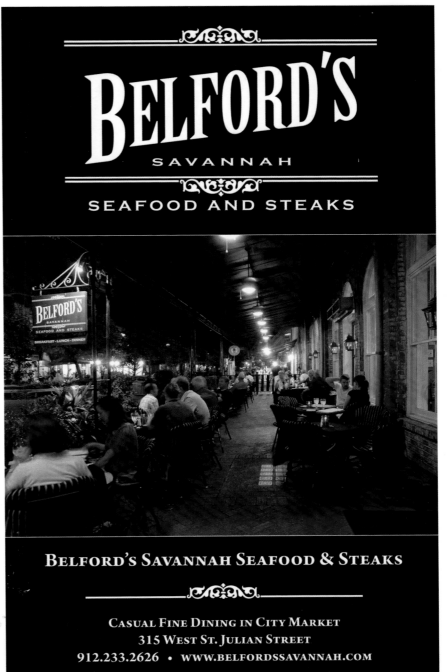

© John Alexander Photography

Love of Food.

No matter where you find your fancy, in Savannah, we love to eat. Whether you're looking for food to go with your live entertainment like they have at Wild Wing Café in City Market or you want to try international food with a Savannah twist like the Greek stylings at Olympia Café, there's something for everyone.

So as you sit down to feast in Savannah prepare to savor every last bite. Because in Savannah, you'll soon discover that food feeds the stomach just as much as it does the soul. ❁

Whether you're in the mood for an experience that's laid-back with live music and cold pitchers of brew or a more sophisticated fine-dining treat, seafood in Savannah is always FRESH!

912.236.7122 | www.17hundred90.com
307 East President Street

Dinner Nightly
5pm - 9pm

Brunch
Saturday & Sunday
11am - 2pm

© John Alexander Photography

In Savannah, you'll soon discover that food feeds the stomach just as much as it does the soul.

SAVANNAH'S CHOICE FOR ISLAND LIVING...

Imagine the exhilarating lifestyle you've always dreamed of. A stunningly beautiful island community where neighbors make you feel at home *before you even arrive*. Golf, boating, sparkling waterways, parks, miles of trails, and a Club that specializes in 'special'. All mere minutes from the historic city of Savannah, Georgia. We've made it a reality at ***The Landings on Skidaway Island***.

Visit and explore: 3 days/2 nights, $249/couple.   TheLandings.com

One Landings Way North   Savannah, GA   SAVANNAH'S CHOICE FOR ISLAND LIVING   TheLandings.com   (800) 841-7011

6 PRIVATE GOLF COURSES—ONE MEMBERSHIP • 40 MILES OF WALKING & BIKING TRAILS • 2 DEEPWATER MARINAS
ACTIVE NEIGHBORS GROUPS • FITNESS & WELLNESS, 34 TENNIS COURTS & 5 POOLS • 4 CLUBHOUSES WITH FARM-TO-TABLE DINING

Celebrate

& Food + Drink
at the Savannah Food *&* Wine Festival

Photos courtesy of the Savannah Food & Wine Festival

If ever there were a time to mark your calendar — this is it.

Each November, for seven remarkable days, those lucky enough to secure tickets indulge in the Savannah Food & Wine Festival. Jam-packed doesn't begin to describe this foodie fairytale come true with more than 40 food-centric events taking place in just one week. From dinners by award-winning chefs in historic mansions to five-star fare in Savannah's squares, the culinary feats are nothing short of magnificent and every bit worth the annual wait.

The roots of the Festival can be traced back to the annual Taste of Savannah, which is now the main event of the Savannah Food & Wine Festival. Produced by the Tourism Leadership Council (TLC), the predecessor event was a one-night affair that brought the very best of Savannah restaurants and the public together for an evening of pure indulgence. That event proved to be such a success that the TLC soon began to generate ideas as to how to make Taste of Savannah more than just one night.

"We wanted to create an event that would benefit our entire community and better serve our membership," commented Michael Owens, TLC President/CEO. "The response has been tremendous and it's exciting to see the impact the festival has made on Savannah's national culinary reputation."

The TLC is certainly achieving its vision with record attendance at last year's event and more than $150,000 raised for various charities. What began as one night has now grown to seven days of one-of-a-kind food and wine experiences specific to Savannah. Attendees come from around the world to get their fill of gourmet indulgence and Savannah's Southern hospitality - but no one can ever really get enough! That's why repeat attendees have become the rule rather than the exception, as hundreds return each year to enjoy edible fantasies old and new.

With each passing year the week's events grow and evolve to keep pace with its droves of devoted patrons. But to give you a glimpse of what may await you at this must-taste festival, gatherings from years past have looked a little something like this...

Celebrity Chef Tour.

This is a night best described as incredibly rare and truly exquisite.

For one evening, award-winning James Beard Chefs combine their extraordinary efforts, each preparing a course for this once-in-a-lifetime dinner. "The Celebrity Chef Tour is the festival's most epic culinary event bringing diverse talents together for a magical, memorable and interactive dining experience," said Owens. Much like dining at the James Beard House, guests of this event have the rare opportunity to interact with the participating chefs throughout the evening.

Grand Reserve Tasting.

If wine is your passion, this is your event!

The Grand Reserve Tasting is the showcase event for the very best wines. Guests are given a collectible piece of fine stemware to use throughout the night (and take home as a souvenir) as they sip a variety of vintages. To round out the evening, a silent auction is also held with such items up for bid as luxury travel, wine and more. So, raise a glass and reserve your tickets to this sell-out event sooner rather than later.

River Street Stroll.

The street where Savannah began, today is the perfect intersection between history and wine.

Savannah's famous River Street is best known for its historic cobblestone pavers, eighteenth-century buildings and sweeping river views. But on this night, the enjoyment of River Street is elevated to an entirely new level. During the River Street Stroll, attendees enjoy an intimate evening of wine and spirits, intermixed with the riverfront's culinary delights and shopping whimsy. It's quite possibly the best way to sip, savor and shop that you'll ever experience!

Taste of Savannah.

Each year this is the main event of the Festival.

So big, in fact, that it has been expanded to **Georgia Railroad Museum** where all do their best to choose from hundreds of wine exhibitors, food booths, cooking demonstrations, celebrity cookbook signings and so much more! Some will come just for the food, others for the cooking demonstrations, while others want to experience it all! You too can take your pick from the many fabulous festivities – that is, if you get your tickets before they sell out!

Jazz & Bubbles Brunch.

What's the best way to cap off an amazing festival? With more food and wine of course! Or in this case – bubbly! Held at the Aqua Star restaurant within the Westin Savannah Harbor Golf Resort and Spa, guests feast on Lowcountry favorites while also enjoying chilled bubbly and the cool sounds of live jazz music. Your eyes may be bigger than your stomach at this event but in celebration of the festival's end, we say, "go for it!" – after all, it will be another year before you eat this well again!

Though the chefs, the food and the wines may change, one thing is certain, every year the Savannah Food and Wine Festival continues to get better and better! Of course that also means it is gaining popularity so it is advised to make your plans early for this can't-miss event by visiting *www.SavannahFoodandWineFestival.com.* Updates are posted regularly as they become available and as history has shown us, the most popular events sell out fast – but trust us, you're going to want to take your time and savor every last bite. **Bon Appetit!** ❁

From dinners by award-winning chefs in historic mansions to five-star fare in Savannah's squares, the culinary feats are nothing short of magnificent and every bit worth the annual wait.

the *Tastes* of SAVANNAH

Nearly 20 years ago, the *Taste of Savannah* became the signature, must attend event to find out what restaurants were THE best places to taste.

Today, the event has evolved into the Who's-Who of Great Tastes. If your trip did not coincide with the festival this year, make plans for next year and enjoy a delectable taste at one of these great restaurants throughout the year.

45 bistro
123 E. Broughton Street
912.234.3111
45bistro.com

Cohen's Retreat
5715 Skidaway Road
912.355.3336
cohensretreat.com

Pacci Italian Kitchen + Bar
601 E Bay Street
912.233.6002
paccisavannah.com

a.Lure
309 W. Congress Street
912.233.2111
aluresavannah.com

Five Oaks Taproom
201 W. Bay Street
912.236.4440
fiveoakstaproom.com

Paul Kennedy Catering
1370 US-80
912.964.9604
paulkennedycatering.com

B's Cracklin' BBQ
12409 White Bluff Road
912.330.6921
bscracklinbbq.com

The Florence
1 W. Victory Drive
912.234.5522
theflorencesavannah.com

Pie Society
19 Jefferson Street
912.238.1144
thebritishpiecompany.com

Belford's Savannah Seafood and Steaks
315 W. St. Julian Street
912.233.2626
belfordssavannah.com

Grand Champion BBQ
Four Atlanta Locations
770.587.4227
gcbbq.com

Savannah Coffee Roasters
215 W. Liberty Street
912.352.2994
savannahcoffee.com

Blowin' Smoke Southern Cantina
1611 Habersham Street
912.231.2385
blowinsmokesavannah.com

Kitchen 320
320 Montgomery Street
912.921.5300
bhotelsandresorts.com

Savannah Square Pops
347 MLK Boulevard
912.999.7078
savannahsquarepops.com

Cha Bella
102 E. Broad Street
912.790.7888
cha-bella.com

Leopold's Ice Cream
212 E. Broughton Street
912.234.4442
leopoldsicecream.com

The Olde Pink House
23 Abercorn Street
912.232.4286

CO
10 Whitaker Street
912.234.5375
eatatco.com

Naan Appetit
1024 US-80
912.348.2446
naanappetit.com

Wild Wing Cafe, City Market
27 Barnard Street
912.790.9464
wildwingcafe.com

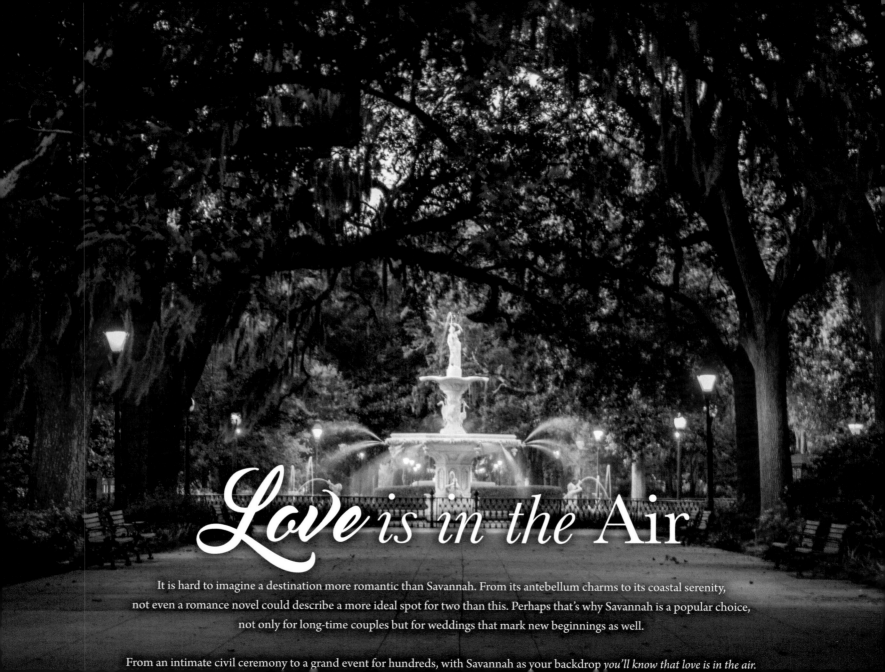

Love is in the Air

It is hard to imagine a destination more romantic than Savannah. From its antebellum charms to its coastal serenity, not even a romance novel could describe a more ideal spot for two than this. Perhaps that's why Savannah is a popular choice, not only for long-time couples but for weddings that mark new beginnings as well.

From an intimate civil ceremony to a grand event for hundreds, with Savannah as your backdrop *you'll know that love is in the air.*

Forsyth Park

At the heart of this picturesque park is the gleaming white Forsyth fountain, making this one of the city's most popular spots for couples to exchange their vows. Not only is the destination breathtaking, it's also convenient, located within minutes of a variety of hotels and reception facilities skilled in catering to your every want and need.

Horse-Drawn Carriages

Just the two of you and the rhythmic sound of horse hooves, taking you on a leisurely tour of Downtown Savannah. You'll find yourself gazing into the canopy of oaks above as you draw closer to the city, and each other on a romantic carriage ride.

© John Alexander Photography

Savannah Philharmonic

For a very special date night, get dressed up for a Savannah Philharmonic performance. This professional orchestra presents a full range of concerts each season (September to May), from classics to pops. Don't forget to eat. Add on a quiet table for two reserved just for you. Whether it's in an historic wine cellar or overlooking River Street, Savannah's dining experience will set the perfect mood for an unforgettable evening.

© Judi Trahan

Squares

Spread out your blanket and picnic lunch, linger in the shade of a Victorian gazebo, cuddle on a park bench and watch the world go by. Choose from Savannah's 22 squares and prepare to get lost in one another.

© Donald Pearson

The Beach

Sunrise or sunset, as the waves gently lap upon the shore, you'll stroll the sands of Tybee Island hand in hand and lose all track of time... best of all, you won't mind one bit. ❀

GOLDEN ISLES®
GEORGIA

To Savannah

95

17

I-95 & Surrounding Areas

25

341

17

Historic Brunswick

520

95

Little St. Simons Island

St. Simons Island

Sea Island

Jekyll Island

One Stunning Location

5 Charming Personalities

Located on the southern part of Georgia's scenic coastline, four barrier islands and the adjoining mainland combine to transport you to a world of serene, natural beauty. Together with fascinating history and recreation of all types, the collection of **St. Simons Island, Sea Island, Jekyll Island, Little St. Simons Island and Brunswick**, will be one of the most captivating places you will ever discover.

St. Simons Island · Sea Island · Jekyll Island · Little St. Simons Island · Brunswick

Goldenisles.com | (800) 933-2627

The Golden Isles is conveniently located just over an hour south of Savannah.

Savannah's
PICTURESQUE PLACES

These days, photos aren't contained to mere photo albums, but shared instantly with the world via any number of social media outlets. The good news is, Savannah abounds with picturesque locales – but it can be hard to narrow them down. Our best advice is to set out on a tour, keep your eyes peeled for these prime points of interests and we guarantee you'll return home with beautiful memories of your Savannah stay.

Teresa House

Forsyth Fountain.

Serving as the backdrop to many a gorgeous wedding, the Forsyth Fountain in Forsyth Park ensures you will capture a stunning photo every time.

Squares.

With 22 squares to choose from, all relatively close together, you will have any number of fountains, gazebos, statues and oak-tree canopies to make even amateur photographers feel like a pro.

© Michael Grafton

© Slarane Springer

© Tracy Woodall

Tybee Island.

Sunrise, sunset and every hour in between, the beaches of Tybee will have you in rapid-shutter mode.

Cathedral of St. John the Baptist.

With its towering dual steeples, ornate architecture and stunning stained-glass windows, this historic place of worship is a must on every photographer's list.

Bonaventure Cemetery.

We know, it may seem a bit creepy, but the ornate headstones and sculptures of this historic resting place may just have you seeing cemeteries in a whole new light.

© Alissa Nicholson

© John Alexander Photography

Isle of Hope.

Just a short drive from Downtown Savannah you'll discover Isle of Hope. With its Martha's Vineyard appeal and Lowcountry charm, this tucked away community is known for its inspired vistas of coastal marshlands at every turn. Be sure to also make a stop at nearby Wormsloe Historic Site offering a breathtaking entry of live oaks and Spanish moss that lead to the tabby ruins of this historic plantation. ❀

You call it
an architectural
masterpiece.
We call it home.

...that's
SAVANNAH
- EST.1733 -

The Mercer
Williams House

 SAVANNAH **HISTORY** MUSEUM   explore history

 SAVANNAH **CHILDREN'S** MUSEUM   play & learn

 OLD FORT **JACKSON**   experience life as a soldier

ATLANTIC STEEL COMPANY
1

 **PINPOINT HERITAGE MUSEUM**   discover life on the water

 GEORGIA STATE **RAILROAD** MUSEUM   ride the rails

CHS A Coastal Heritage Society Experience
www.chsgeorgia.org

What do YOU want to do?

You've made it to Savannah! Now, what do you want to do?

Savannah has an endless array of choices. Packed with history, entertainment, interaction and knowledge, you'll find something to do around every corner. Here are some of our favorite things to do!

Ride a Locomotive
655 Louisville Road | 912.651.6823 | chsgeorgia.org/roundhouse

Thomas the Tank Engine would have felt right at home at the Roundhouse Railroad Museum, where a giant turntable still shifts cars onto tracks. Little engineers can learn about the history of steam engines and belt-driven machinery, and model train buffs will kick up their heels at the huge display of downtown Savannah! The museum is open daily, but train rides are seasonal—call ahead to check the schedule.

© Colleen Thompson

© Margo Sullivan

© Margo Sullivan

Explore A Fort

U.S. 80 Hwy E. | 912.786.5787 | nps.gov/fopu

As you walk through the cannonball-shattered walls of Fort Pulaski National Monument, it's a cinch to imagine what it was like to guard the Savannah River way back when. Built in 1847, the fort was used by Confederacy and thought to be impenetrable until the Union Army tested its new rifled canon in 1862, rendering brick forts everywhere obsolete. After you've strolled through both levels, check out the visitors' center's films and live demonstrations as well as the moat, drawbridge and network of wooded trails. Keep your eyes peeled for a deer or a bald eagle—or, considering its haunted reputation, maybe even the ghost of a Confederate soldier.

© Telfair Museum

© Telfair Museum

Be an Architect

207 W. York Street, Savannah | 912.790.8800 | telfair.org

Build a likeness of one of Savannah's historic homes or create something no one's ever seen before with the blocks at ArtZeum at Telfair Museum's Jepson Center for the Arts. The two-level, 3500 square-foot gallery has plenty more to keep little hands busy, including a magnetic sculpture wall and interactive exhibits using works from the Telfair collection.

See Science in Action

30 Ocean Science Circle | 912.598.2496 | marex.uga.edu

The scientists at the UGA Marine Education Center and Aquarium on Skidaway Island are delighted to share their findings with visitors. A premier marine science research facility, the educational complex features 14 saltwater aquaria, interactive exhibits and a wheelchair accessible boardwalk around the marsh.

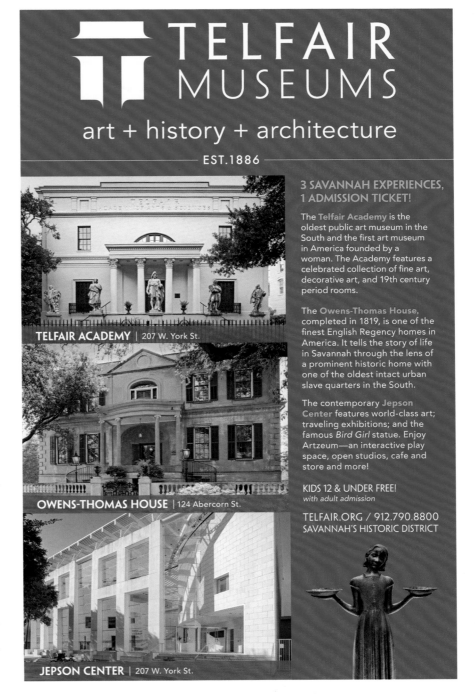

Fly a Helicopter

1125 Bob Harmon Road | 912.247.0047 | oldcityhelicopters.com

Take the ride of your lifetime aboard a small yellow helicopter. Fly low and fast along the Savannah River while you enjoy a unique perspective of downtown Savannah, Old Fort Jackson, Fort Pulaski, Whitemarsh Island, the Cockspur, and Tybee and Hilton Head lighthouses. The views are spectacular!

Touch a Sand Dollar

1510 Strand Ave., Tybee Island | 912.786.5917

tybeemarinescience.org

Depending on the day, the touch tank at the Tybee Island Marine Science Center is swimming with creatures native to the Georgia Coast, including whelk, hermit crabs, starfish and more. Learn about the tides, reefs, dolphins and life cycles of sea turtles that nest on our local beaches. The center also offers guided beach walks, marsh treks and gift shop full of fluffy critters to take home!

Explore an Outdoor Museum

655 Louisville Road | 912.651.6823 | chsgeorgia.org/SCM

Explore and play outside in this two-level, outdoor play ground. The museum is entirely outdoors and features over a dozen exhibits designed to expand the imaginations of children including an exploration maze, a reading nook and a sensory garden.

© Savannah Children's Museum

© The Pirates' House Restaurant

Dine with Pirates

20 East Broad St. | 912.233.5757

thepirateshouse.com

Legend has it that Captain Flint from the Robert Louis Stevenson classic "Treasure Island" died in an upstairs room at what is now The Pirates' House Restaurant with first mate, Billy Bones, at his side. This landmark eatery opened in 1753 as an inn for seafarers. Keep your eyes open for pirates in the dining room ready to pose for photos between courses!

Ride a Ferry

3 stops; Trade Center, Waving Girl and City Hall

connectonthedot.com

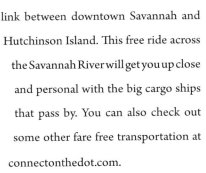

© Savannah Food & Wine Festival

The beloved Savannah Belles Ferry system offers a unique alternative to the Talmadge Bridge as a link between downtown Savannah and Hutchinson Island. This free ride across the Savannah River will get you up close and personal with the big cargo ships that pass by. You can also check out some other fare free transportation at connectonthedot.com.

© Old Fort Jackson

Let Your Ears Ring

1 Fort Jackson Road | 912.232.3945

chsgeorgia.org/jackson

Hear the awesome thunder of cannon fire at Old Fort Jackson, one of only eight "second system" fortifications built prior to the War of 1812 still standing in the U.S. The Coastal Heritage Society maintains the visitor's center featuring an exhibit of historical weapons and a host of highly-entertaining guides dressed in period garb.

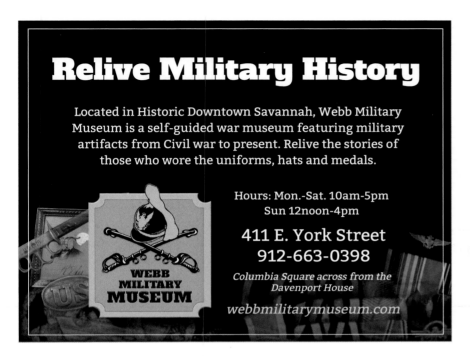
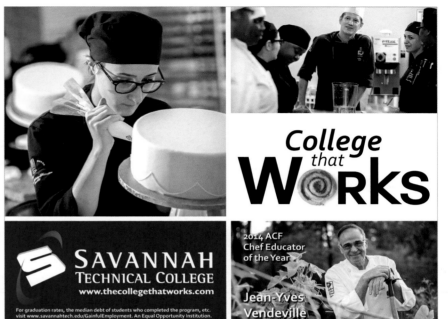

Treasure Hunt Hidden Gardens

41 Martin Luther King Jr Blvd. | 912.232.1511 | shipsofthesea.org

Folks in Savannah take pride in their gardens, and there's a treasure trove of hidden gems around town. Go in search of some of these beauties, but remember, most of them are private gardens, so look but don't touch. And, if you want to explore one of the city's most beautiful gardens first hand, visit the museum garden at the Ships of the Sea Museum. It's beautiful no matter what the season, and offers a place to meditate, relax and soak in the beauty that surrounds.

Nose to Nose with Nature
711 Sandtown Road | 912.395.1212 | oatlandisland.org

Just minutes from downtown, the Oatland Island Wildlife Center allows you to get up close and personal with nature as you take an easy two-mile nature trail that winds through lush Lowcountry forest and serene marsh. You'll see wolf, alligator, wildcats, bison, owls, eagles and farm animals. ❋

Savannah's SCREENS

As you make your way through our breathtaking settings, you might be getting a little déjà vu. Chances are you've seen our cobblestoned streets, natural beaches and historic homes on the silver screen. Or, maybe you've seen the effects of some of our well-known characters. Either way, as you're moving around Savannah, be camera-ready because you just might hear, "lights, camera, action."

© Timothy Liley

Films

Baywatch: Dwayne Johnson, Zac Effron, Priyanka Chopra *(2017)*

Dirty Grandpa: Robert De Niro, Zac Efron, Zoey Deutch *(2016)*

The Birth of a Nation: Gabrielle Union, Armie Hammer, Aja Naomi King *(2016)*

The Do Over: Adam Sandler, David Spade, Luis Guzman *(2016)*

Gifted: Chris Evans, Jenny Slate, Octavia Spencer *(2016)*

Magic Mike XXL: Channing Tatum, Jada Pinkett Smith, Amber Heard *(2015)*

The SpongeBob SquarePants Movie 2: Clancy Brown, Tom Kenny, Bill Fagerbakke, Carolyn Lawrence *(2015)*

The Conspirator: Robert Redford, director with Justin Long, Evan Rachel Wood & Robin Wright Penn *(2009)*

The Last Song: Miley Cyrus, Greg Kinnear *(2009)*

The Gift: Cate Blanchett, Keanu Reeves, Katie Holmes *(2000)*

The Legend of Bagger Vance: Matt Damon, Will Smith, Charlize Theron *(2000)*

Forces of Nature: Sandra Bullock, Ben Affleck *(1999)*

The General's Daughter: John Travolta *(1998)*

The Gingerbread Man: Kenneth Branagh, Embeth Davidtz, Robert Downey, Jr. *(1997)*

Midnight in the Garden of Good and Evil: Clint Eastwood, director *(1997)*

Something to Talk About: Julia Roberts, Dennis Quaid *(1995)*

Now and Then: Demi Moore, Rosie O'Donnell, Melanie Griffith, Rita Wilson & Christina Ricci *(1995)*

Forrest Gump: Tom Hanks, Sally Field *(1994)*

Glory: Denzel Washington *(1989)*

The Longest Yard: Burt Reynolds *(1974)*

Cape Fear: Gregory Peck, Robert Mitchum and Polly Bergen *(1962)*

Celebrities

Paula Deen: *(1947 -)* This iconic restaurateur, cookbook author and TV personality got her start on the southside of Savannah making box lunches for nearby offices.

Clarence Thomas: *(1948 -)* A Justice of the Supreme Court of the United States, Thomas is the second African American to serve on the Court.

Charles Coburn: *(1877-1961)* An Academy Award® winner, Coburn was an actor much beloved for his comedic roles and smooth low voice.

Flannery O'Connor: *(1925-1964)* A writer of the dark but humorous Southern Gothic genre, she is also known to have trained a chicken to walk backwards at her Savannah home on East Charlton Street.

Johnny Mercer: *(1909-1976)* Arguably the most famous and beloved of all Savannahians, four-time Academy Award® winner Johnny Mercer was a prolific singer and songwriter and co-founder of Capitol Records.

Juliette Gordon Low: *(1860-1927)* Juliette founded the Girls Scouts of the U.S.A. Her birthplace in Savannah is a favorite spot among scouts young and old.

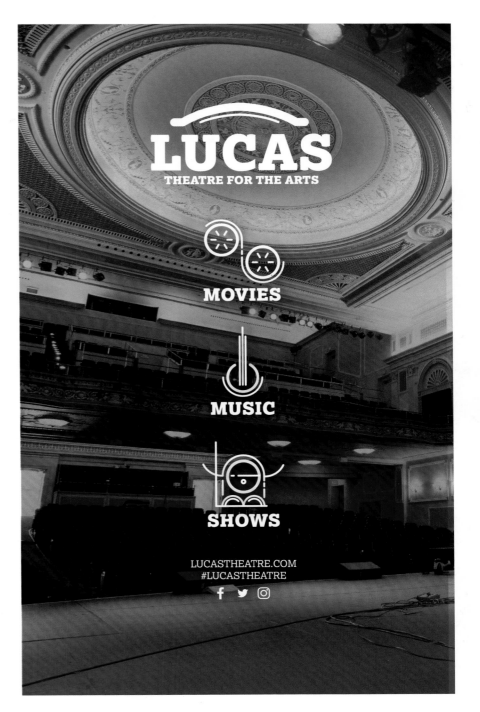

LUCASTHEATRE.COM
#LUCASTHEATRE

CITY ✺ MARKET

Where City Activity Meets Local Creativity

BELFORD'S
SAVANNAH
SEAFOOD AND STEAKS
BREAKFAST - LUNCH - DINNER

© Kevin Banker

Within this unique marketplace there is always something new to encounter, something different to find and something hidden to uncover. You may have to look around a corner, behind a door or up a remote staircase, but that's part of the charm that makes City Market so special.

Since the early 1700s, City Market has been the commercial and social center of historic Savannah. Located on the original site of the market used by farmers and traders of all kinds to sell their goods and wares, City Market offers the best of what is old and new in Savannah.

Today, Savannah's City Market comprises a four-block area of restored warehouses and shop fronts adjacent to Ellis Square. This charming, open-air marketplace houses a wealth of things to do, whether you come for the entertainment, to shop, dine or just relax a moment and rest your weary feet.

Savannah boasts a vibrant art scene and City Market is at the center of it all. As you visit City Market, allow plenty of time to enjoy the wide variety of art galleries – from fine art to contemporary art – featuring more than 50 local artists. An especially unique experience offered at City Market is the Art Center, where you can watch artists create original works in their studios.

City Market is also home to some of the best places to eat in Savannah. Diners can satisfy their appetites at one of the many restaurants, cafes or specialty food shops located within steps of one another. The options will appeal to all tastes and pocketbooks with a casual atmosphere and outdoor dining that are available just about year 'round. If a sit-down meal isn't on the menu, you can still sample City Market's best by simply enjoying an ice cream, espresso or cocktail in the public courtyard while watching people pass by.

© Patrick McGhie

© John Alexander Photography

You may have to
LOOK AROUND A CORNER,
BEHIND A DOOR *OR*
UP A REMOTE STAIRCASE,
but that's part of the
charm that makes
CITY MARKET
so special!

© John Alexander

© Tim Welch

© Tim Welch

© Geoff Johnson

The mercantile and produce offerings of yesteryear in City Market have been replaced by an eclectic blend of art galleries and specialty shops. Shoppers will discover unique gifts, original works of art, freshly made candy and a host of other delights at the many shops and boutiques that welcome visitors to browse and buy.

© John Alexander Photography

© Tim Welch

Entertainment in Savannah abounds and City Market is certainly a hub for fun things to do. Outdoor entertainment, including street musicians, live music and special events, is featured in the pedestrian-only courtyards of City Market almost daily throughout the year. Indoor entertainment is also provided year 'round by many of the restaurants and bars throughout the market. As the evening nears, City Market's tucked-away nightspots offer a variety of enticing cocktails to cap off a spirited night on the town. Whether on the rooftop or on the lower level of the courtyard, you're sure to find a place that suits your preference. Additionally, carriage and trolley tours leave and return to City Market each day making it the perfect embarkation point to explore more of our beautiful city.

a one-of-a-kind place where **past & present** *beautifully combine...*

Though the farmers and merchants from centuries past may have never envisioned the City Market of today, it is their entrepreneurial spirit that has enlivened this unique place into the bustling epicenter of activity that it has become. Without a doubt, City Market offers visitors a one-of-a-kind experience in a one-of-a-kind place where past and present beautifully combine to create a truly local must-see Savannah attraction.

EXPERIENCE CITY MARKET

City Market is not a place you visit. *It's a place you discover and explore.* A place that's **romantic**, **historic**, **serene** and **exciting**. You may have to look around a corner, behind an old door or up a remote staircase. But that's just part of the charm and what makes City Market so special.

 CITY MARKET
THE ART & SOUL OF SAVANNAH

912.232.4903 • SavannahCityMarket.com
JEFFERSON AT WEST ST. JULIAN STREET

 ART CENTER
SAVANNAH

A COMMUNITY OF 35 WORKING ARTISTS
WHO MAKE AND SELL THEIR WORK IN A
SERIES OF STUDIO LOFTS AND GALLERIES.

SAVOR... Savannah

A unique & memorable venue
for your special day.

Experience the
Starland District
South of Forsyth Park, a Creative Neighborhood of Local Goodness

The Vault Kitchen & Market
2112 Bull Street
912-201-1950
The Vault Kitchen and Market is a renovated local banking institution turned industrially chic eatery.

Back in the Day Bakery
2403 Bull Street
912-495-9292
A Southern American Bakery serving breakfast, lunch, good coffee and other delectables to the neighborhood.

Starlandia Creative Supply
2438 Bull Street
912-417-4561
Reclaimed art and creative materials store for artists, artisans, and creators of all ages, talents, and dreams.

Foxy Loxy Cafe
1919 Bull Street • 912-401-0543
A specialty coffee house and bakery serving Tex-Mex inspired fare.

The Vicar's Wife
2430 Bull Street • 760-828-0902
A unique vintage store with fabulous furniture, jewelry, lighting, artwork, and gorgeous gifts.

Canine Palace
2805 Bull Street • 912-234-3336
Pet supplies, premium dog and cat foods. Anything your dog or cat could dream of!

Starland Cafe
11 E 41st Street • 912-443-9355
Delicious and fresh sandwiches, soups and salads. Open for lunch daily.

Wax & Wane Waxing Salon
1917 Bull Street • 912-233-7002
Head to toe hair removal services specializing in hard wax, male and femaie brazilians, and brows.

House of Strut
17 W 41st Street • 912-712-3902
Psychedelic-chic vintage fashion for the fun and eclectic family. Great prices and amazing selections.

Sulfur Studios
2301 Bull Street • 912-231-7105
Multimedia space including artist studios, gallery space, workshops and more.

Graveface Records & Curiosities
5 W 40th Street • 912-335-8018
New and used vinyl as well as toys, games, taxidermy and more! The only curated record shop in town.

The Florence
1 W Victory Drive • 912-234-5522
Neighborhood restaurant that highlights local and regional ingredients using Italian techniques and backgrounds.

Gypsy World
2405 Bull Street • 912-704-2347
Vintage boutique located in heart of the Starland District. Apparel and accessories for men and women.

Savannah's Art Side

Beyond the city's historic homes and museums, one of the best ways to get to know Savannah is through its artistic side, which can be explored inside galleries that beautifully encapsulate past, present and future.

First Friday Art March in Savannah's Starland Art District

Indie Arts Market, Desoto Avenue between 40th and 41st Street | 912.376.9953 | artmarchsavannah.com

If you want to know where the locals are on the first Friday of every month, you'll find them in Savannah's trendy, artsy neighborhood on the First Friday Art March. It's a free monthly, self-guided tour of Savannah's Starland Art District south of Forsyth Park.

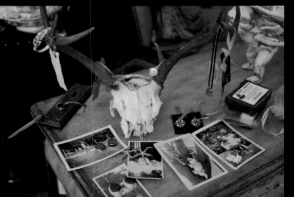

The Art Center at City Market

Jefferson St. at W. St. Julian Street | 912.232.4903 | savannahcitymarket.com

Traditional and contemporary influences meet sparkle and whimsy among the dozens of galleries and studios that make up this community of artists and craftsmen. Observe painters, sculptors and textile artists at work in dozens of studios. There are even more galleries along City Market's open-air walkways—an entire day can be spent exploring this historic site known as "The Art and Soul of Savannah." Free and open to the public.

The Australian Aboriginal Art Gallery

404 W Broughton Street | 912.436.6625 | theaustralianaboriginalartgallery.com

Explore art from the oldest living culture in the world at the Australian Aboriginal Art Gallery with mesmerizing works of art. This is the only gallery on the eastern seaboard specializing in contemporary Aboriginal Art. There's a range of original artworks, from small affordable works to large investment pieces, by some of the most renowned Aboriginal artists in the world.

Roots Up Gallery

6 East Liberty Street, Parlor Floor | 912.677.2845 | rootsupgallery.com

Roots Up Gallery specializes in showcasing the works of local artists and will provide you with a one-of-a-kind souvenir. You'll also discover a wonderful array of paintings, sculptures, pottery and jewelry from local and regional artists.

Savannah College of Art & Design Museum Of Art

601 Turner Boulevard | 912.525.7191 | scadmoa.org

A world-renowned art and design school makes finding art in this city easy. Check out the rotating exhibits at the SCAD Museum of Art, where you'll see works from students and masters alike. The exhibits rotate on the school's quarter system.

Savannah's Business Side

We all know Savannah is a beautiful destination city for you to visit, but what about combining training and education into your trip? The savvy traveler can gain more than just rest and relaxation while visiting, why not consider all of the educational opportunities our hostess city provides.

Georgia Tech Savannah

If you want to find some great career-advancing, skill-developing classes while you're in Savannah, check out the Georgia Tech Savannah Leading Well Workshop Series. These two-day workshops get at the heart of what you need to know about becoming an exceptional leader. If they don't have a workshop while you're here, it's well worth planning another trip back to Savannah.

Savannah Technical College

If you want to try your hand at a new career altogether, you could look at Savannah Technical College for professional continuing education classes, they offer everything from facility management to fly fishing. These classes are generally more than a day, and require someone who's going to be here for a few weeks. So, settle in and get to learning.

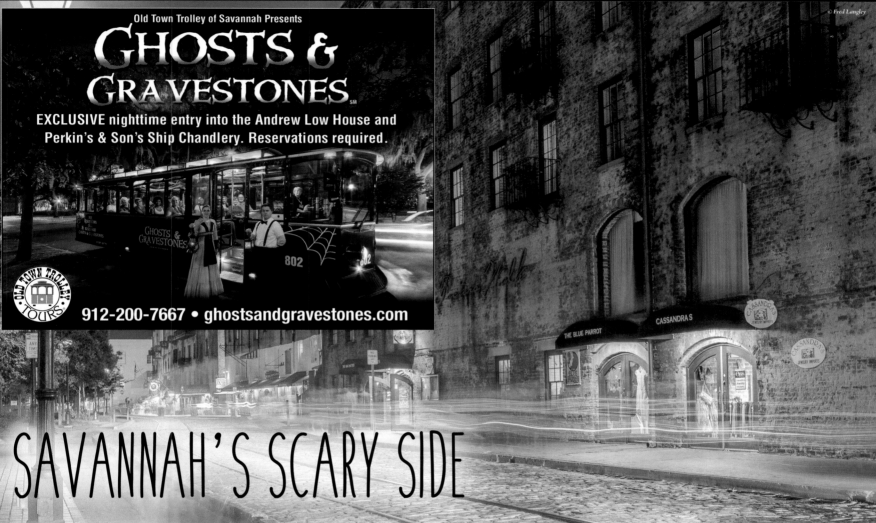

SAVANNAH'S SCARY SIDE

The Pirates' House

Underneath this famed restaurant are the remains of one of the oldest buildings in Savannah. The deeper you go, the creepier it becomes with tunnels that run from the basement to the Savannah River, where many a sailor met his fate at the hands of merciless pirates.

Madison Square

During the American Revolutionary War, the Battle of Savannah was fought in the area known as Madison Square. Shadowy figures are said to roam this square and many believe them to be soldiers who were slain on this very ground.

River Street

This retail and restaurant mecca was once home to warehouses and ship docks dating back to the very founding of Savannah. With a history like that, there's bound to be a lingering ghost or two peering out on the cobblestone streets.

10 Reasons to Check Out
RIVER STREET

This cobblestoned stretch is a favorite place to pick up a perfect souvenir, enjoy a sumptuous meal, watch a taffy pull or hop on a trolley ride to explore more than 100 shops, restaurants and pubs. *Here's a host of facts about Savannah's riverfront you may not know.*

1 *It's a multicultural wonderland.* Throughout the year, River Street hosts family-friendly festivals from Oktoberfest, featuring lederhosen and wiener dog races, to Blues, Jazz & BBQ with its tasty treats and sultry sounds. And of course, there's the largest St. Patrick's Day celebration in the country, when everyone becomes Irish for the day just for showing up.

2 *You can sit with history – literally.* Nestled above the river level on Yamacraw Bluff on the property of the Hyatt Regency Savannah is a Mediterranean-style rounded white bench created by the Colonial Dames in 1905. The bench marks the exact spot General Oglethorpe pitched his tent to rest his first night after docking in the new colony on February 12, 1733.

© Joey Gaston

© Cindy Hornung

© Donald Pearson

© Erin Kelly

3

The night sky crackles with color regularly.

Fireworks elicit "oohs" and "aahs" every first Friday of the month when Savannah Waterfront Association puts on a fabulous show of pyrotechnics and live music. Artisans line the plaza with their distinctive works, and many shops stay open late on First Fridays.

4

The nation's fourth-busiest container port lies just up the river.

The Georgia Ports Authority handles millions of shipping containers from all over the world, and many of the goods that hit everyone's favorite stores around the country passed through Savannah first.

5

The city's finest music plays under the moonlight.

At most of the festivals that call River Street home, you'll find local bands that range from Southern Rock to Smooth Jazz. With a built-in, open-air stage, you're sure to find your sound. And, if you don't, walk a few steps more to hear some of the talented live musicians.

6

The ends of the earth are under your feet.

Savannah's early developers recycled the ballast used on ships to pave the streets, laying cobblestones originally quarried in Canada, the British Isles, France, Spain and beyond. Still solid—and charming—after almost three centuries, the varied materials of River Street (as well as some of the retaining walls and structures) include limestone, granite, quartz and basalt.

7

A famous girl waves you closer.

Look closely for the statue. Do you see her? That's Florence Martus also known as "the Waving Girl." She took it upon herself to be the unofficial greeter of all ships that entered and left the Port of Savannah between 1887 and 1931. Her undying spirit lives on with everyone who will greet you along the way

8

Pirates once docked on these shores.

Lore has it that sea-faring outcasts and plunderers—including the fearsome Bluebeard—made liberal use of Savannah's old inns and pubs in the 18th and 19th centuries. The old tunnel at the Pirate's House Restaurant emptied out near the river, where unsuspecting sailors plied with rum were shanghaied onto waiting vessels and forced into pirate life.

9

Docking didn't come easy.

The high bluff made for good anchorage for early ships, but the steep bank and treacherous currents proved challenging for loading and unloading passengers and supplies in the city's early days. Savannah's wharves benefitted from the Industrial Revolution when equipment powerful enough to drive concrete piles into the river bottom was brought in, creating easy access for large vessels. You can still see the public wharf towards the east end, constructed in 1872 for smaller boats.

10

Shopping hasn't changed much in a few hundred years.

You can peruse the wares of more than a hundred merchants up and down River Street, just like Savannah shoppers did when the road was little more than a bumpy route. Today's delicacies include sweets from River Street Sweets and Savannah's Candy Kitchen.

Legendary Golf

Coastal Cuisine

Free Water Ferry

heavenly spa
BY WESTIN

Heavenly Spa

Crafting Cocktails

Whether you're in need of a cool drink in the warmth of summer, or something with some kick to warm you from the inside out, there's definitely a cocktail for that. Better yet, Savannah laws allow you to take that drink with you in a to-go cup so you're sure not to miss a thing! Drinking in all that Savannah has to offer includes bellying up to the bar and raising your glass to one fantastic getaway.

Chatham Artillery Punch

This is one cocktail that is not for the faint of heart – or the really thirsty - since it is best enjoyed after chilling in the refrigerator for two days. Its namesake is part of history as it is known to possess a kick greater than the two brass cannons presented to the Chatham Artillery by George Washington. Feeling brave *(or a little crazy?)* here's how to mix a batch yourself! - >

Mint Julep

If you want the quintessential Southern cocktail, this is it. The ingredients are seemingly simple: bourbon, fresh spearmint, distilled water, granulated sugar and powdered sugar. The preparation, however, is best left to a professional bartender since it involves soaking the mint leaves, making simple syrup and then 'muddling' the concoction with a mortar and pestle. Much easier to order, don't you think?

Savannah Tea

Long Island isn't the only city known for an adult libation. In Savannah, we serve ours with sweet-tea-flavored vodka, gin, rum, triple sec, tequila, lemon juice, cola and lemon-lime soda. So refreshing, you will lose all track of time *(and how many you had).*

CHATHAM ARTILLERY PUNCH

(be sure to invite some friends over for this one!)

1 ½ gallons Catawba wine
½ gallon rum
1 quart gin
1 quart brandy
½ pint Benedictine
2 quarts Maraschino cherries
1 ½ quarts rye whiskey
1 ½ gallons strong tea
2 ½ pounds brown sugar
1 ½ quarts orange juice
1 ½ quarts lemon juice

Mix from 36 to 48 hours before serving.

Add one case of champagne
when ready to serve.

*(and more importantly, don't plan on going
anywhere after bottoms up!).*

© Jason Manchester

Remembering
YOUR TRIP

Wish you could extend your stay in Savannah? We do. We love having you here, but if you have to go home. Be sure to take a piece of Savannah with you.

Remember your trip to Savannah with one of these fabulous finds.

© Hilton Head Island Chamber of Commerce

© Aimee Brubelow

Gullah Straw Basket

Culture, function and beauty combine in these handcrafted creations that are a signature of the Lowcountry. The art originated in Sierra Leone, West Africa but was handed down to descendants of enslaved African people, known as Gullah; a tradition that continues to this day.

Antiques

With a city this old, we have hundreds of years worth of antiques for you to treasure. Whether you find a beautiful tapestry or your new favorite table, there are so many reasons to check out our antique stores. And, many of them will ship to your home, so you're not stuck trying to fit it in your carry-on luggage. One of our favorites is Victory Antiques in midtown.

Jewelry

LEVY *Jewelers* SINCE 1900

With every gem wrapped in a signature navy box, you know Levy Jewelers will make your remembrance of Savannah unforgettable. After all, this family has been providing the community with jewelry for 117 years. It's a true Savannah staple with its flagship building in the Broughton street shopping district

Georgia Wine

Before America was a sovereign nation, the British had eyes on Georgia as the wine capital of the new colonies. Nearly 300 years later, we're celebrating our rich wine history with some spectacular local wines. Share our hidden secret with your loved ones.

Savannah Book

What's the best way to share your Savannah experience? With a book that starts the conversations with friends about your wonderful trip. Local book retailers are peppered throughout the city where you can pick up your favorite version of this book, *Savannah: A Southern Journey*. Or, just order your own copy at TourismLeadershipCouncil.com.

WHATEVER THE *Weather*

An integral part of any Savannah visit is getting outdoors.

Experiencing all of Savannah's natural allure is, of course, best enjoyed when the weather is at its finest.

And while we may heat things up in the summer, on average you'll have every reason to seize the day with Savannah's inviting temperatures ready to greet you year round.

© Aaron Brumbelow

© Aaron Brumbelow

© Aaron Brumbelow

© William Levitt

When it Rains

As a general rule, it's always best to start your day in Savannah early.

Rains tend to be late in the day and the heat can become a little intense during the summer months for outdoor activities after lunch. All Savannah tour companies consider the weather when planning their tours and many schedules are built to enjoy Savannah during the most inviting times of the day.

What to Wear

If you're wondering what to wear in Savannah, comfortable shoes are definitely a must.

In fact, your whole suitcase might just consist of lightweight fabrics, unlined jackets, a hat and an umbrella. Other than something a bit dressier for a special dinner or a sweater first thing in the morning, when it comes to packing for Savannah, the weather is so pleasant it's just that easy.

Cooling Off

It does get "cool" in Savannah at certain times of the year – even downright cold for a day or two.

January is Savannah's coolest month but even so, the average afternoon highs still reach the 60-degree mark. There have been those rare occasions, however, when the city has been as cold as 3-degrees back in 1985 but the very next day it was up to 68 by the afternoon. Thanks to the effects of the nearby Atlantic Ocean, Savannah's cold snaps never last long.

Beat the Heat

Warm summers are a given in Savannah.

July tends to be the warmest month but it's also a great reason to seek out some fun "relief" on the beaches where the ocean's waters remain cooler than the air temperature. There have been triple-digit record setters in the past, some as hot as 105-degrees in 1986, but summer also brings Savannah's greatest average rainfall to cool things off, usually in locally heavy late-day thunderstorms.

© William Levitt

VISIT TYBEE

Wake up to the waves. Savor it all. Leave the rest behind.
A 20-minute drive is all it takes.
VisitTybee.com

Visit Tybee Island
SAVANNAH'S BEACH

SAVANNAH'S *Sandy Side*

Seeing the historic sites in Savannah may require a good pair of walking shoes, but just 20 minutes east of the city, you'll discover another great escape that is best experienced barefoot – Tybee Island, Georgia. Unlike many coastal beaches, which are dotted with high-rise condominiums and theme parks, the people of Tybee Island have made it their mission to retain the island's vintage charm, providing a truly laid-back year-round vacation experience.

Perhaps that's why Tybee Island has been named one of *Southern Living's* "Perfect Beach Towns," just one of many accolades the island receives year after year. *Parents* magazine has recognized Tybee as one of America's "Best Beaches for Families," while *Fodor's* has honored the island as one of the "Best Family Beaches on the East Coast."

With a history that dates back to the eighteenth century, complete with lore of pirates and buried treasure, Tybee's five miles of sandy public beaches officially became a resort destination in 1887. At that time, Savannah's wealthy would visit the island, known as the community of "Ocean City," arriving by train or by steamship. Fast forward nearly 40 years and Tybee's palm-lined highway, which remains the island's sole access route to this day, makes it easy for beach-goers to bask in the warmth of the Southern sun.

© Michael Graton

Once you arrive on the island, if your idea of the perfect beach day includes planting a chair in the sand for hours on end, Tybee offers ample opportunity to do just that. You can opt for a quiet secluded stretch of beach on the north side of the island, or the daily attractions near the scenic Tybee Island Pier on the south side. For those who prefer a more active experience, Tybee also offers dolphin tours, deep-sea fishing excursions, kiteboarding lessons, kayaking, jet skiing, paddle boarding and more. Of course there's also the unique souvenir shopping on Tybrisa Street at the north end of the island, with its one-of-a-kind art galleries and great gift shops.

Another must-see while visiting Tybee is the Tybee Island Light Station. Built in 1773, the Tybee lighthouse is the oldest and tallest in Georgia. Climb the lighthouse's 178 steps and you will experience a breathtaking birds-eye view from atop the lighthouse. After your inspiring climb, you can also enjoy the Tybee Museum and gift shop, which are both located on the premises.

Now that your exercise is done, it's time to eat! In keeping with its nostalgic feel, many of the restaurants on Tybee are also long-time establishments whose owners know how to cater to Tybee locals and visitors alike. Fresh seafood abounds at Tybee eateries where you can easily get swept away by the island's fun atmosphere and ocean breezes.

But the fun doesn't stop there. Tybee Island is also famous for its annual celebrations, where strangers are sure to become fast friends. Pull out your water guns and get soaked at the Beach Bum Parade, which officially heralds the beginning of summer over Memorial Day Weekend, and watch the magical Independence Day Fireworks display over the ocean in July. In February,

© Bill Anderson

© Annie Nemeth

© Michael Grafton

© Tim Welch

© Bill Anderson

© William Levitt

© Michael Grafton

Both Southern charm and a commitment to preservation run deep on the island.

you can practice bead catching during the Mardi Gras celebration followed soon after by the opportunity to flaunt your green best at the Irish Heritage Parade in celebration of St. Patrick. For a swashbuckling good time, the whole family will love the Tybee Island Pirate Festival parade in the fall where there's no shortage of fun.

Tybee for the Holidays also offers plenty of family-friendly activities from Thanksgiving to New Year's Day. Ring in the New Year with a spectacular fireworks display and brace yourself for the Tybee Polar Plunge, which offers a refreshing dip in the Atlantic Ocean on New Year's Day.

As you set foot on Tybee you're sure to notice that both Southern charm and a commitment to preservation run deep on the island. From renovated vintage beach cottages to the newly-restored historic Tybee Post Theater, the island continues to be the perfect complement to Savannah.

Without a doubt, as you feel the sand between your toes and hear the crash of the waves, looking out over a horizon that stretches as far as the eye can see, you, too, will be swept up in the authentic beach town of Tybee. *All we can say is, join the club!*

© William Levitt

SAVANNAH'S *Comfort* FOOD

Every region has its own version of "comfort food" and the south is no exception.
Here are just a few of the local favorites sure to make anyone feel right at home.

FRIED GREEN TOMATOES

First, you pick unripe, green tomatoes from the vine, then you slice them to a medium thickness, dredge them in buttermilk, coat them in cornmeal and a little salt, and fry them to a golden brown. *If you've never tried them, we think this Southern side will soon be one of your go-to favorites.* They are often served with a dipping sauce that can be a remoulade or other mayonnaise-based sauce.

SHRIMP & GRITS

When you're this close to the coast, shrimp and grits are a no-brainer. Wild-caught Georgia shrimp are a staple in this area, and when placed atop of creamy cheese grits, this is a delicious combination you have to try.

PRALINES

You simply cannot leave Savannah without savoring a melt-in-your-mouth praline. Made with pecans, brown and white sugar, corn syrup and evaporated milk, pralines are like sweet caramel with a bite! Made even better by the crunch and sweetness of pecan pieces scattered throughout. *No wonder we Southerners are so sweet!*

GRITS

To Southerners, grits are as common as rice, but to some out-of-towners, they are a bit of a head scratcher. Simply put, grits are small broken grains of dried corn. Depending on how finely ground they are, you can prepare grits as a side dish or as a coating used for baking and frying. *Breakfast, lunch or dinner, grits are a delicious, creamy addition to any meal.*

HOE CAKES

Folklore states that these corn-based pancake-looking staples got their name because they were baked on the blade of a gardening hoe by slaves in the field. Made from cornmeal, water and salt, hoe cakes have crispy edges with a dense yet creamy inside. *Eat them as a side topped with butter and maple syrup or use them to help sop-up every last bit of good food on your plate.*

LOWCOUNTRY BOIL

Another dish that plays on our proximity to the coast, lowcountry boil mixes shrimp, crab legs and smoked sausage with ears of corn and new potatoes. All the ingredients are boiled in one big pot and seasoned with a delicious blend of spices. *This dish is often served on a table with newspaper, so don't be afraid to get your hands dirty!*

FEELING *Festive* IN SAVANNAH

Savannah is undoubtedly an exciting mix of cultures and traditions that can best be enjoyed at the city's many annual festivals. From celebrating the Irish at the world's second-largest St. Patrick's Day parade to watching an explosion of Independence Day fireworks in a beautifully historic setting, we encourage you to make your plans now for a festival-filled and unforgettable year to come. To make the most of your planning, it's best to contact each festival for specific event information as dates and scheduling changes may occur.

© Timothy Lilley

Martin Luther King Jr. Parade & Celebration

(January - February)

The dream of Dr. Martin Luther King, Jr. is still alive and well in Savannah thanks in large part to the MLK Jr. Observance Day Association, Inc. Each year the Association plays hosts to a series of events in honor of this visionary leader for civil rights, all culminating in a grand parade with more than 300 entrants annually. Prior to the January parade, an Annual Gospel Festival and Musical Salute to Dr. King are just a few of the events available as part of this momentous celebration. In February, events such as the Annual Dr. King Freedom Ball and Memorial Scholarship Awards dinner beautifully pay tribute to Dr. King by celebrating the past and investing in the future of promising college students. For more information and to reserve your seat at the many hosted events, please be sure to check the Association's website.

© John Alexander Photography

Savannah Book Festival

(February)

The Savannah Book Festival invites you to *"lose yourself in books!"* at its annual event hosted in historic downtown. This is the ideal opportunity to getaway for a long weekend in Savannah as the festival hosts various events for a selected Thursday through Sunday each February. Attendees will have the opportunity to hold one-on-one discussions with best-selling authors, gain insight into the writing process and secure a signature or two from icons of the written word. Throughout the four days, guests can choose from any number of simultaneous author presentations occurring at venues throughout downtown Savannah, most of them free and open to the public. Selected events do require tickets for a minimal price so be sure to check the festival's website often for schedule and author information. If you've been looking for a festival to write home about – this is it!

© John Alexander Photography

St. Patrick's Day
(March)

Savannah's largest and most attended event is the annual St. Patrick's Day Parade and Celebration. More than just a day, St. Patrick's Day in Savannah is a citywide event where the population more than doubles in size as genuine and honorary Irish descend on the city. This time-honored Savannah tradition first began in 1813 when a small group of Hibernians formed their own parade through the streets of Savannah in memory of Patron Saint, Saint Patrick of Ireland. Today the parade has grown into a three-hour feast for the eyes and ears as military divisions, high-school bands and bagpipers from all over the world descend upon our city.

Though the parade is the main event, the celebration actually begins two weeks prior to St. Patrick's Day with festivities such as the greening of the fountain in Forsyth Park, Tara Feis and the Savannah Irish Festival to name a few. River Street and City Market are also hosts to their own St. Patrick's Celebrations where good-hearted reverie fills the streets and a spontaneous party atmosphere can be enjoyed from dawn to dusk and beyond. Just know, if you happen to be served a breakfast of green grits and eggs, they are perfectly fine – just part of the spirit of St. Patrick you can only enjoy but once a year!

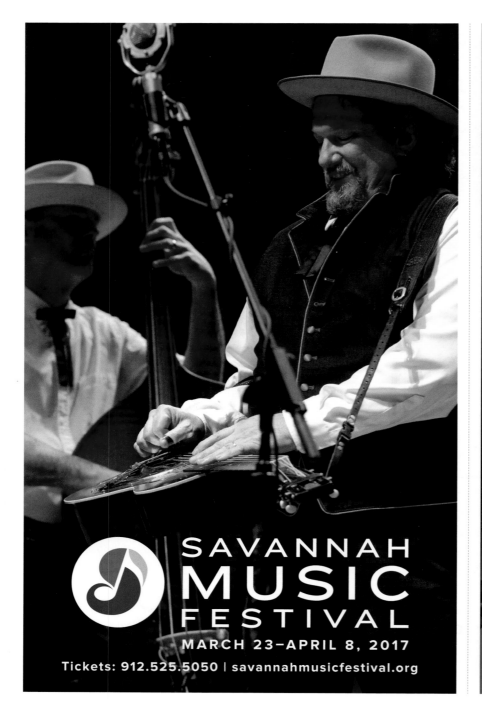

Savannah Music Festival
(March - April)

Each spring, against a background of blooming azaleas and temperatures just right for a night out on the town, the Savannah Music Festival puts on an unforgettable event. As the largest musical event in Georgia and one of the most distinctive cross-genre music festivals in the world, the Savannah Music Festival is a world-class celebration of the musical arts. The saying, "there's something for everyone" definitely applies. Previous festivals have welcomed a range of talents and musical types, from Emmylou Harris to the Atlanta Symphony Orchestra, Bela Fleck to Lyle Lovett, Jazz with Wynton Marsalis to Curtis Blackwell & the Dixie Bluegrass Boys – you're sure to hear from artists you love and discover new ones along the way. Since its beginning in 2003, the Savannah Music Festival has continued to grow in popularity and size as evidenced by its years of record ticket sales. So be sure to plan ahead and secure your tickets early for a musical celebration like no other.

© Savannah Music Festival

July 4
(July)

Surrounded by the history that is Georgia's First City, you're sure to experience a July 4th celebration that is as exciting as it is inspiring. Each year on Independence Day, River Street is the place to be to witness the illumination of fireworks in the night sky reflected in the waters of the Savannah River below. Standing on Savannah's historic cobblestones with thousands of your newest friends, you're sure to smile at the collective "oohs" and "ahhs" of the crowd, gathered together in honor of freedom.

In fact, July 4th in Savannah is so widely celebrated that you have two opportunities to watch an amazing fireworks display. The day before the festivities on River Street, nearby Tybee Island plays host to thousands of beachgoers who hang around until the sun goes down for an ocean-side seat to the annual pyrotechnics show. Each year on July 3rd, Tybee Island sets the Atlantic Ocean aglow as attendees recline in the sand to watch fireworks overhead. Go once and you'll be hooked, making Independence Day in Savannah one of your favorite must-do annual traditions.

© John Alexander Photography

Savannah Voice Festival

(August)

There is perhaps nothing more beautiful than the sound of a pitch-perfect voice in song. The Savannah Voice Festival agrees and that is why organizers gladly bring the city together for a weeklong event of diverse and engaging voice programming. Led by opera legend Sherrill Milnes and his wife, soprano Maria Zouves, the Savannah Voice Festival features opera, musical theatre and song interpreted by more than 50 classically trained emerging artists. Though the core of the festival is held during a selected week each August in Savannah, SVF offers audiences a chance to attend a variety of concerts throughout the year, including National Opera Week in the fall among others. Surrounded by the history and romance of Savannah, lost in the beauty of angelic voices, the Savannah Voice Festival provides attendees a getaway for mind, body and spirit.

 There is perhaps nothing more *beautiful* than the sound of a pitch-perfect voice in song.

Tybee Island Pirate Fest

(Late October)

Arggghhh you ready to have some pirate fun? Then make your plans today to attend the Tybee Island Pirate Fest. Located just 20 minutes east of historic Savannah, Tybee Island transforms into a pirate's fantasy for three swashbuckling-filled days. Every Columbus Day weekend, attendees of the Pirate Fest enjoy live music and family-friendly activities all hosted at Tybee's South Beach parking lot, located on Tybrisa Street. Grownups can quench their thirst at the Pirate Pub with live music, while the kiddos enjoy a petting zoo, Ferris wheel and even a costume contest (great for adults, too). There's so much more to experience at this celebration of the Georgia coast that you have to see it for yourself! So, grab your best pirate garb and reserve your spot – Columbus Day weekend will never be the same!

© John Alexander Photography

Savannah Film Festival

(October - November)

Have you always wanted to attend an exclusive film screening? Or wondered what really goes into the editing process (and on the cutting-room floor)? Maybe you want to learn about the future of special effects, animation and filmmaking? Then this is your chance to ask industry experts everything you want to know - up close and in person. For eight glorious days each fall at venues throughout downtown Savannah, the Savannah College of Art and Design (SCAD) presents the Savannah Film Festival. With attendance upwards of 40,000 people, SCAD brings Hollywood to Savannah offering a variety of workshops, panels, lectures, special screenings and competition film screenings. This wildly entertaining event is made possible by the creative contributions of both award-winning professionals and also emerging student filmmakers. Whether you've always wanted to break into the film industry or you're a die-hard movie buff ready for an unprecedented behind-the-scenes pass, you'll need to make your reservations now to ensure a front-row seat is ready and waiting.

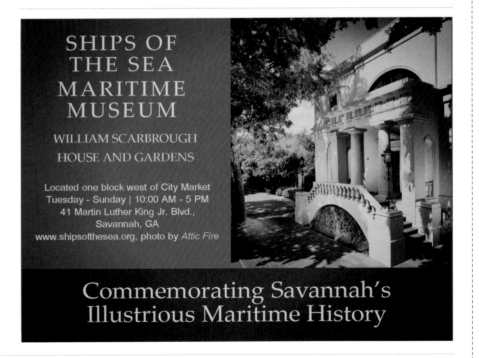

The annual Savannah Film Festival is your chance to ask film industry experts anything & everything you want to know - *up close and in person.*

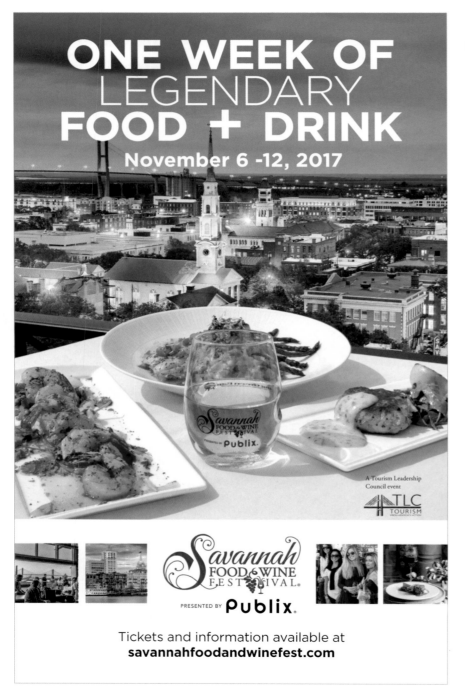

ONE WEEK OF
LEGENDARY
FOOD + DRINK
November 6 -12, 2017

A Tourism Leadership
Council event

TLC
TOURISM

Savannah
FOOD & WINE
FEST&IVAL®
PRESENTED BY **Publix**®

Tickets and information available at
savannahfoodandwinefest.com

Savannah Food & Wine Festival
(mid November)

If ever there were a time to mark your calendar – this is it. Each November, for seven remarkable days, those lucky enough to secure tickets indulge in the Savannah Food & Wine Festival. From dinners by award-winning chefs to five-star fare, the culinary feats are nothing short of magnificent and every bit worth the annual wait. The roots of the Festival can be traced back to the yearly Taste of Savannah, which is now the main event of the Savannah Food & Wine Festival. What began as one night has now grown to seven days of one-of-a-kind food and wine experiences specific to Savannah – and every foodie's dream! Past Festivals have featured such events as a River Street Stroll where attendees can taste wine, sample culinary delights and shop at the same! There are also celebrity chef gatherings and the main event, the Taste of Savannah, which features entertainment, live cooking demonstrations, children's activities and more. Attendees flock to this annual event from around the globe and as the saying goes, "the early bird gets the worm" –or in this case, the wine and gourmet meals! It's advised to reserve your space sooner than later.

> From *dinners by award-winning chefs* to *five-star fare*, the culinary feats are nothing short of *magnificent* & every bit worth the annual wait.

Year-Round River Street Festivals

No matter what time of year, River Street has a festival to celebrate: Arts and crafts, entertainment and fun abound during First Saturday celebrations, and the German culture and songs of Oktoberfest, the greenest St. Patrick's Day celebration in the nation and Fourth of July Fireworks always draw a crowd. Events are always open to the public! We encourage you to visit www.riverstreetsavannah.com for details.

Moving
to
SAVANNAH

For those who can't get enough of Savannah,
here's how you turn your vacation into a
remarkable relocation.

© William Levitt

While the history and beauty of Savannah is likely what brought you here, it is the city's hospitality that will make you want to stay. Thankfully, the city and its nearby communities offer a magnificent choice of neighborhoods that will soon have you wanting to put down some permanent roots.

© Bill Anderson

Wilmington, Whitemarsh & Tybee Island

Wilmington and Whitemarsh Islands feature a mix of estate-home communities as well as ranch-style homes and a variety of luxury apartments and condominiums. Nearby Tybee Island is best known for its beach cottages that will beckon you to slip off your shoes, sink into the sand and stay awhile.

The Landings

Located on Skidaway Island, this private, gated community is less than a 20-minute drive from downtown but feels worlds away. Home to six world-class golf courses, 34 tennis courts, two marinas (with access to the Intracoastal Waterway), four clubhouse restaurants, 40 miles of trails and a newly renovated 48,000-square-foot fitness center, the Landings offers superb Savannah living.

Midtown

Made up primarily of the Ardsley Park neighborhood, Midtown Savannah is iconic for its homes with Belgian block walls and Spanish-style roofed pillars that are as architecturally stunning today as when they were first constructed in 1909. Ardsley Park features many small parks that are neighborhood gathering places and beautiful focal points with playgrounds, picnic areas and a ball field.

Southside, West Chatham & Beyond

For communities featuring newer construction, you'll find abundant options in Southside Savannah as well as areas just beyond the city limits including the up-and-coming community of Pooler. Outside Chatham County, Richmond Hill and Rincon are two great communities that are a stone's throw from Savannah.

© John Alexander Photography

Isle of Hope

Picture white picket fences and expansive coastal views and you will have envisioned Isle of Hope. This quaint island features a variety of home styles that combine to form a truly authentic coastal community.

Historic Downtown

From historic homes remodeled to look like new, to new homes constructed to fit in with Savannah's historic appeal, living downtown puts you close to all of Savannah's culture and activity. To help hone in on your favorite locale, we recommend dividing your search into downtown's four well-known sections including the Historic Landmark District, Victorian District, Thomas Square/Starland and Baldwin Park. All of these neighborhoods will put you within walking and biking distance of some of Savannah's most iconic attractions. Who wouldn't want to stroll by the Forsyth Park Fountain every day?

© Kate Bagoy

THE DAY OF A *Lifetime*

HILTON HEAD ISLAND
South Carolina

Just over the bridge from Savannah, you'll enter a world where nature's beauty and resort luxuries coexist like nowhere else on earth. On Hilton Head Island, rich Gullah Heritage, born of a culture more than two centuries old, is yours to explore. Dine, shop, renew your sense of inner peace and still make it back to your room in time for turndown service. As long as you promise next time, you'll stay a little longer.

South Carolina
Just right.

HILTONHEADISLAND.ORG | 800-523-3373 | 🐦 @HILTONHEADSC | 📘 FACEBOOK.COM/VISITHILTONHEAD | 📷 VISITHILTONHEAD

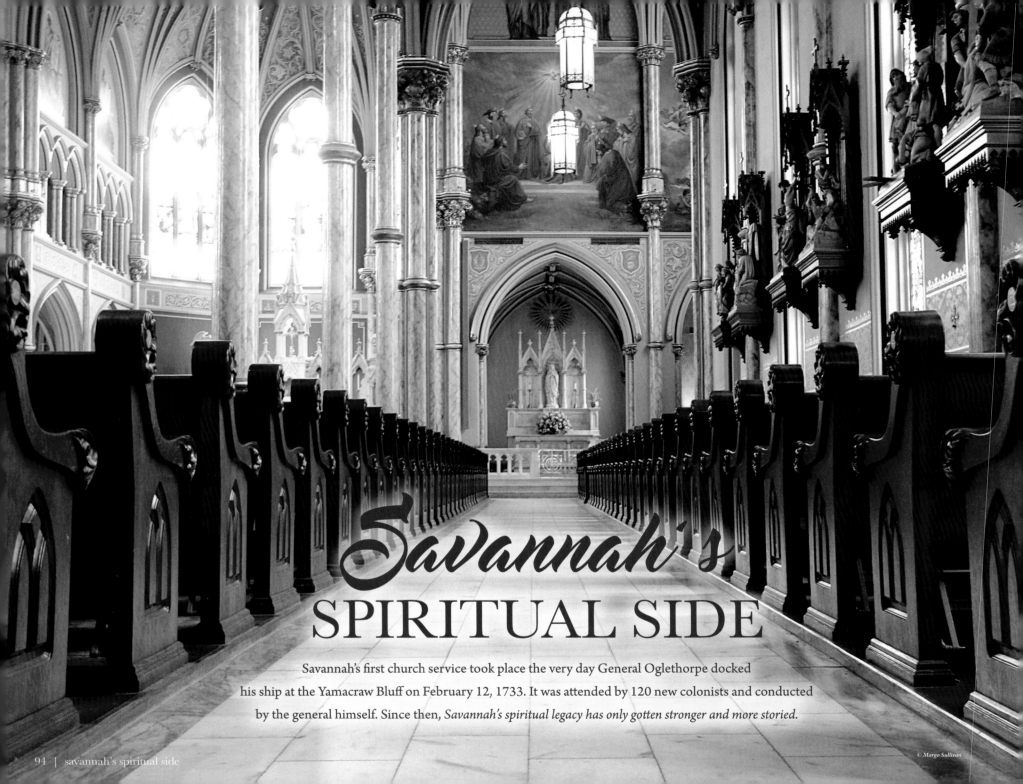

Savannah's SPIRITUAL SIDE

Savannah's first church service took place the very day General Oglethorpe docked his ship at the Yamacraw Bluff on February 12, 1733. It was attended by 120 new colonists and conducted by the general himself. Since then, *Savannah's spiritual legacy has only gotten stronger and more storied.*

© Margo Sullivan

First African Baptist Church & First Bryan Baptist Church

FAB: 402 Treat Avenue | 912.232.8981 • FBB: 575 West Bryan Street | 912.232.5526

Savannah is home to America's oldest African American church, though two lay claim to the distinction. Both First African Baptist Church and First Bryan Baptist Church trace their roots back to Andrew Bryan, a baptized slave who founded the first ordained black Baptist church in 1788. The congregation split in 1832 with one retaining the name and the other the original building.

St. John the Baptist

222 East Harris Street | 912.233.4709

In 1799, the city's ban on Catholicism was lifted and permission was granted for the construction of St. John the Baptist. The stunning cathedral that stands today on Harris Street was dedicated in 1876.

© Shauna Johnson

© Patrick McGhie

Congregation Mickve Israel

20 East Gordon Street | 912.233.1547

A few months after the colony of Savannah was established, the English ship William & Sarah brought a group of 41 Jewish travelers, mostly of Portuguese origin, to Savannah. They became the Congregation Mickve Israel, which is still operating as the third-oldest congregation in the nation, occupying one of the country's only Gothic synagogues.

© Bryan Stovall

© Lydia Duarte

© BAPS Swaminarayan Mandir

BAPS Swaminarayan Mandir

355 Canebrake Road | 912.920.2121

Honoring the Hindu faith and preserving the Indian culture in Savannah, the BAPS Swaminarayan Sanstha temple provides a welcome space for visitors to quiet the mind or learn arts, language, music, and philosophy. They're open most days of the year including bank and federal holidays.

editor in chief   Molly Swagler

creative director   Abbi Carter Gravino

advertising   Ron Scalf

contributing writers
Jesse Blanco, Laura Clark, Heather Grant, Angela Hendrix,
Allison Hersh, Jessica Leigh Lebos, Christine Lucas, Tim
Rutherford, Claire Sandow and John Wetherbee

photographers
John Alexander, Bill Anderson, Kate Bagoy, Aaron Brumbelow,
Melissa Cooper, Lydia Duarte, Rodney Gary, Joey Gaston,
Michael Grafton, Cindy Hornung, Teresa Houze, Geoff Johnson,
Casey Jones, Erin Kelly, Fred Langley, William Levitt, Timothy
Lilley, Jason Manchester, Patrick McGhie, Annie Nemeth, Alissa
Nicholson, Donald Pearson, Sharon Springer, Bryan Stovall,
Margo Sullivan, Colleen Thompson, Judi Trahan, Benjamin
VanDuin, Tracy Woodall

publisher: Tourism Leadership Council
Michael T. Owens, President & CEO
Molly Swagler, Vice President
Hallie Mobley Anderegg, Director of Operations
Claire Sandow, Communications Coordinator
Ron Scalf, Member Services & Sales Manager

© 2017 Tourism Leadership Council

Published by the Tourism Leadership Council
www.tourismleadershipcouncil.com
P.O. Box 10010, Savannah, Georgia 31412

ISBN 978-0-692-80529-9

Printed in Canada.

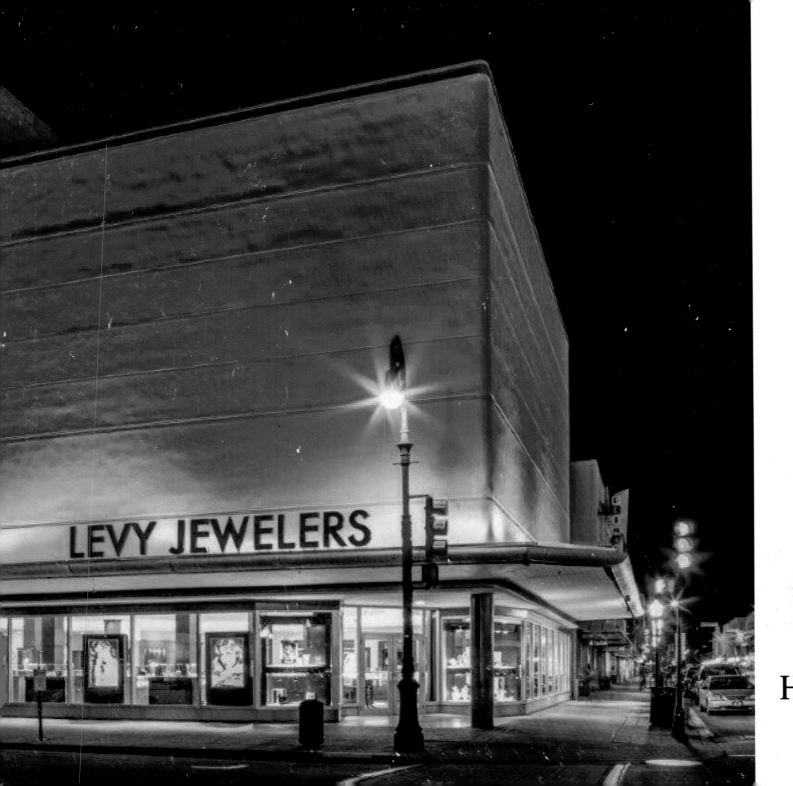

MIKIMOT

BREITLIN
· 1884 ·

Historic Downtow